Mom.

A COLLECTION OF PERSONAL AND POIGNANT
JOURNEYS TO MOTHERHOOD

JULIE CANGIALOSI

NIKKI NOYA

For all moms and for the women still waiting for their rainbow

Foreword

CATHERINE RINGLER

I have had the honor of being called Mom for many years and have recently added Grandmama to my list of monikers. I have been blessed with two beautiful daughters, Julie, and her older sister Kelly, both easily conceived putting me at a distinct disadvantage while witnessing Julie's difficult journey towards her lifelong dream of motherhood.

To simply say I am proud of the woman she has become would be an unforgivable understatement. I remain in absolute awe of her courage, conviction, and commitment to helping others go after their dreams.

Like the other courageous woman featured in this book, who have so generously shared their personal stories of tragedy and triumph, you my darling daughter, fill my heart with inspiration.

Introduction

When you look up the definition of mom you will find "one's mother" in The Oxford English Dictionary or "female parent" in Webster's. Our personal definition of mom is usually emotional, sometimes complex, but always unique. So too is the road to motherhood.

This book is compiled of testimonials from Moms across the country. They have shared their stories of love, heartbreak, joy, loss, surprise, and everything that truly defines being a MOM. Period.

CHAPTER 1

Julie

I t was an out of body experience, and to this day when I close my eyes I relive the very moment our lives changed forever.

Let me rewind our story to the beginning (well almost the beginning). My husband James and I always loved a sense of adventure and travel and were fortunate enough to travel quite a bit. When we were first struggling with infertility we stopped making major plans including travel far out in the future because we always said "what if".... what if I am due then? Would I want to travel that far? Is that a good location to take a baby? Well, after over a year we stopped the "what if's" and started planning. We made plans for a welcome distraction and the realization that not everything can be planned. So we booked a dream trip on our bucket list to Bora Bora and a few other Islands in French Polynesia.

We were well in our second trimester so we had the all clear from our medical team, hearing his heartbeat many times including the day before we left. In the middle of our trip I just didn't feel right, I couldn't put my finger on it, the Dr later told me it was mother's intuition. We went to see a doctor at the clinic on the island. To this day I can still hear the sounds of the monitors in the clinic, I can still see my husband's face filled with worry, grief and sadness and I can still see the doctor in his wrinkled lab coat mouthing the words, "I am sorry the baby is gone." In that moment I couldn't hear or comprehend the words he was saying. I was in denial that we lost our son, Charlie. The next week continued to be a blur.

Once I was physically healed and we traveled back home, I could finally begin my mourning process but I honestly didn't know where to start. So I started by writing down all of my questions, feelings, and thoughts. I really struggled with the limited resources available and I longed for answers. My doctor didn't have many either but was so encouraging that we had a less than 1% chance or losing another child in the second trimester. It was with that faith, our love and hope that we tried again.

Unfortunately, for us we were met again with another tragedy when we lost our daughter Lena. Losing two children within 16 months completely shattered our lives, especially mine.

During that time our friends seem to all have babies, I felt like I was literally at a baby shower each week. Sitting in the back of the room with a "fake" smile drinking mimosas. I was happy for my friends but still secretly grieving so attending the events was so difficult. In retrospect I wish I politely declined some, when I was just simply not ready.

Still looking for answers on our journey our OBGYN suggested we get information from Dr Kliman in Connecticut. At that time he was one of the few physicians that would preform an autopsy and hopefully provide the answers we were so desperately seeking. When we received results we found out that there was a problem with my placenta and I have a chromosomal abnormality I never knew I about. An inversion or chromosome number 9. I immediately became depressed while my husband went into action mode. Our fertility specialist in DC told us that we had 2 options "designer IVF" or try again naturally and maybe this time the chromosomes will align correctly. When you meet me you know I like most things designer but it was still a new approach almost a decade ago and I just was not sure I wanted to travel to Dallas or NYC for a designer baby, at least not yet. Dr F. gave us anecdotes of his patients who were just like me and went on to have multiple miscarriages and others who had multiple children naturally. It was truly up to us on what we wanted for our next step. James wanted to try IVF because he was not sure he could see me suffer again with a second trimester loss but I said I have "one more in me." He begrudgingly said OK.

Almost 6 months later, the day after my birthday, I saw the 2 pink lines again. I was over the moon that my birthday wish came true but then almost immediately my excitement turned to fear. All the "what if's" came through my head....

Each week at my ultrasound appointment I would hold my breath as I would say a prayer. When I heard my favorite sound each week I would relax for a moment and feel peace. At our 20 week scan I asked the doctor when I could relax? His response: "20 weeks ago." I laughed for a second realizing that the best thing I could do for my son was to relax and try to enjoy the pregnancy. I would sing and read to him daily.

Apparently he was so cozy he wanted to stay inside the womb longer and my water finally broke at 40 weeks and 4 days. After 47 hours of labor we finally met our son, Landon August. Two years and almost two weeks later we met our daughter Elle Rose.

I never imagined how long our journey would be to

become parents but I am so proud to be a mom of four; Landon, Elle and our 2 guardian Angels, Charlie and Lena.

Never wanting parents to feel alone on their journey I have spent the past 8 years helping couples just like us through various organizations.   James and I were also called to start our own 501(c)(3) non profit: Operation Little Angel 101: Hope After Loss.   We wanted to help couples who are suffering in silence everyday after the loss of a child. The angelic message of 101 is faith, strength and hope. Our mission is to value and celebrate the life shortened by miscarriage, stillbirth or early infant death while honoring and supporting families in their grief.   We provide education, resources and tangible cuddle boxes or as I like to call them a warm hug when you need it most.

CHAPTER 2

Nikki

Before I knew what Gonal-F was, how much I hated Lupron, what Menopur feels like, I had a dream about my future daughter Samantha. Before the word adoption had even crossed our minds, or the countless doctors visits and heartbreaks, I saw her in my dreams so clear- ly. A beautiful girl with curly hair in a school uniform dancing and twirling around, so happy. Now that Sam is almost 5 and our family is complete, I think back on those days when I tried so hard to get pregnant and one day be A MOM. My IVF journey brought me so close and connected to so many other women, from all different backgrounds and situations, all going through this process. I found strength, compassion, support and love from other women that went through it, were going through it, that had been successful and those that had not. The power of women when they get together is..incredible.

After 3 rounds of IVF my body could not take anymore. I felt defeated, like a failure, hopeless and confused. I'm healthy, I'm an athlete, everything I set my mind to happens! WTF?! I must have walked across the Key Biscayne Bridge 300 times to clear my mind and find some peace. I wanted to be a mom, so much, to my core.

My last round of IVF failed in June of 2017, and on August 9th we got an email telling us a birth mother had chosen us to adopt her unborn baby, due in November. That woman is my hero. She let me be in the room when Samantha was born, she let me cut the umbilical chord, she let the doctors put the baby in my arms first. She gave me the gift of motherhood, and this book is dedicated to all women on their journey. We each have different stories, and sharing those stories here gives that love, support and strength I was given those years ago. I am finally a Mom.period.

Please find my journal entries from this important time in my life below.

Sept 29, 2015

Today is the day we started looking for you. We have tried before, but something is not quite right. We don't know what it is yet, but we know you are close. Everyone at The Fertility and IVF center in Miami was amazing, I loved Natascha and Larissa. They tried to take my blood but my vein collapsed and I almost passed out! Your father was charming and perfect of course, had no problems and everyone fell in love with him. I am so happy we started today. I am so ready to meet you.

October 12, 2015

I started my period early today, and just for a slight moment I thought maybe, just maybe it was you. Then I scheduled my HSG test and started watching videos of women recounting their experiences and had a TOTAL MELT-DOWN. Apparently it is very painful and I just got completely overwhelmed and scared. But I know I have to do this. Your dad was so amazing today. So was LUKA. They sat in my office with me and held me so tight and let me cry.   I have another blood test Wednesday with my favorite Natascha so hopefully I will get some clarity and questions answered.

October 14, 2015

Great Dr. appointment today. I'm getting better at having my blood drawn for sure. I have to lie down, and I have to squeeze the shit out of the puffy thing the nurse gives you. All of my blood work came back negative , which is great news, and all my genetic testing was negative-yay. The nurse Teresa then spent QUITE a bit of very uncomfortable time looking for my ovaries-even going so far as to asking if I had any..........??? .....Wow.............but the good news is both my ovaries had follicles! YAY. The next step is the HSG test which I had a meltdown about. But mommy got a valium and hopefully will be just fine. I'm nervous but this has to be done. I've wrapped my head around this process and am feeling calm. Looking for my ovaries today really was not fun, but your father stood next to me the whole time and let me hold his arm-very hard. Today we also re-enforced I am not flexible at all.

October 21, 2015

Yesterday was the highly dreaded HSG test....I am so happy that is over with. Lying by myself in that cold, sterile hospital room for so long only made my anxiety of the pain to come that much worse. Luckily I had an awesome doctor that I really liked. Magda made the whole experience that much better, and really calmed me down. And the valium. Then the margaritas helped too. I got wasted at Smith and Wollensky. Very, very drunk.

November 2, 2015

Had meeting with Dr. Jacobs today to go over all tests results. Looks like I have to have a small surgery soon to remove polyp and check for endometriosis. I'm totally overwhelmed after today. I do really like Dr. Jacobs, but listening to all that's ahead made my head spin. I had a good cry in the parking lot of the Dadeland mall on such a hot November day. I'm really not even nervous for the surgery, I'm nervous to start the IVF. But I can do this. I'm determined.

November 17, 2015

Tomorrow is the surgery. I am so ready for this to be over. I haven't slept in days and am feeling like I am the reason you are not happening. I just want to get this over with. I'm willing to do whatever it takes.

November 19, 2015

Recovering at home now from surgery. Everything went very well, but wow the anesthesia has kicked my ass. I was so sick last night and feel like I've been hit by a truck. The good news is I have a perfect uterus! The nurses at the center were so amazing I really can't explain what a difference they made. Kenny has been the best nurse and Luka has not left my side since I got home. I'm already on the mend and ready to enjoy the holidays. I'm scarred and sore, but it's done. I'm so happy that is over with!

January 1 , 2016

Tomorrow I start day 1 of the IVF journey. I had a complete meltdown at my doctors appointment the other day after they explained how to do all the injections. It was way too much information at one time, I was very overwhelmed and scared. Started to cry in the parking lot, I needed Kenny there. I felt alone and scared. Then when I got home I proceeded to fracture my foot. Then as I 'm getting X-rays at the hospital , I start my period. Needless to say, it was a lot. I haven't been sleeping and am in a lot of pain. It being the holiday is not helping either. Everything is closed, I'm alone and just feeling like I'm barely hanging on. As soon as I get my cast on, a scooter, and start I will be fine. It's just a lot at once. The universe is telling me to slow down.

January 10, 2016

So we've hit another setback. At my last Dr. appointment they didn't like the way the cyst on my left ovary looked. Soooooo, now I'm on birth control pills to dissipate the ovary. Yep, a broken foot and on birth control pills. This has been such a difficult time, I feel trapped, helpless, agitated and restless. I have another dr. appointment in a week , which means hopefully I only have to take these pills for another week.

January 18 2016

Ok, the demon pills seem to be working. Left cyst gone. Going back Saturday morning to see about right one. Lets do this

February 3 2016

My stubborn right cyst did not go away. Not after 3 weeks of demon pills and 10 days of psycho progesterone pills. I was so up set I cried. Dr Jacobs then aspirated the cyst, which was intense. Very intense. It felt like someone put on cleats then kicked me square in the goods. Traumatizing!

Now I'm waiting for my period to come to go back and more blood tests more ultrasounds but hopefully we can start injections soon.

Feb 4-15, 2016

Ok so the morning Lisa and Marie got here Feb 4th bloodwork came back and we started injections. Having them here was actually a great way to start I was very nervous. Every morning and evening Kenny and I sit at the dining room table while we prepare the injections. We started at 2 in the morning, 2 in the evening now we are 3 in the morning, double menopur and 2 at night. We have now been to the doctor 3 morning in a row for bloodwork and ultrasounds. The good news is I'm growing follicles!

I have such a pouch and am very tired all the time but it looks like we could be doing egg retrieval as soon as this Wednesday. YES!! I hope so, I am over this phase....the injections are ok, its uncomfortable but I have surprised myself with what I am capable of. Also, I could have done none of this if it weren't for the amazing support of Kenny. He has truly been a wonderful husband throughout this emotional rollercoaster.

February 20, 2016

Thursday February 18th was finally egg retrieval day. I, of course, did not sleep a wink the night before and I was so anxious. All the nurses were great and everyone stopped by to check on me. Dr. Jacobs was able to retrieve 6 eggs and the next day the office called to tell me 4 were successfully fertilized. I want to break into the lab right this minute and see them. I'm praying for them to stay healthy and grow strong. We hear from the dr office tomorrow to learn about the progress. For now I am just ridiculously bloated, tired and uncomfortable but hopefully it will go away soon!

March 7, 2016

Day 5 after egg retrieval we got terrible news. The embryos were not strong enough to survive and were growing abnormally. The drs decided not to proceed with testing and we were told I am going into early menopause and maybe we should consider donor eggs.............To say I was devastated would be an understatement. I do not know if I have ever felt so low in my entire life. After all that, all the shots, blood tests, ultrasounds, excitement, drs appointments, planning, waiting, pills, mood swings, bloating, happiness, sadness, it all came to sitting in the backyard all day and crying. We are deciding to take a month off to heal and start again in April. I'm not giving up. I am emotionally drained but I am very strong, and I have Kenny to hold me up.

April 30 2016

Have been on Estrace for a week and got terrible period. This morning was first injection of Lupron and it HURT. It hurt so much I cried it burned and felt like I got punched. I felt like I was at the bottom of a mountain too high to climb. The real fun starts Monday......

May 6, 2016

Just home from the dr....

The Lupron shots SUCK. It's very painful

But, it seems the follicles are growing. I'm so swelled up and bruised. I'm cautiously optimistic. Up to now 6 injections a day of demon juice Lupron, menapur and gonal. 3 in the morning and 3 in the evening.

May 10, 2016

3rd day in row of blood tests, ultrasounds, feeling so bloated none of my clothes fit me, so tired I don't feel like doing anything and more waiting......I am so ready for this to be over. I feel like a trapped tiger.

I have to remember not to lose sight of what we are actually doing here, but it is very difficult especially since this is round 2. I have to be calm, this phase is almost over. This will be the last time I am doing this. I am very strong, but the emotional, physical, mentally, spiritual toll this process takes is too much, even for me.

May 13, 2016

Home from the hospital and egg retrieval. I think I heard them say they got 12........? I haven't heard yet and am dreading the phone call. I feel ok, very tired, and crampy, but the actual procedure was good. The anesthesiologist was amazing and I really like Yanet the nurse. I am so bloated and brusied. I'm ready to get back to myself-pregnant or not. And I'm ready for FUN!!!

May 22, 2016

Out of 12, 2 were successfully fertilized, but did not make it. I'm exhausted. I'm spent. I feel depleted and tender everywhere. I know in my heart I did everything I possibly could to grow healthy eggs this round. I rested, I ate well, I drank so much coconut water I never want to see another coconut again. I don't know where to go from here. I don't want to do this again.....I don't know if I can do this again. It is so mentally, physically, emotionally, spiritually exhausting. And expensive. UGH And I feel terrible. Through it all I have the best husband ever. I could not have done this without him. He truly loves me unconditionally. Sometimes I have to go for a very long walk because I get so cranky and agitated and its like I have level 10 PMS allll the tiiime. We are going to take this summer, relax and go home to Lakeville. So it continues, but just a different way

October 25 2016

What a summer.....Norman passed away and we are just getting back to Miami. We had an appointment with Dr Jacobs this morning and are thinking of starting round 3 in January...............we also reached out to Heart of Adoptions so lets do this! I would really not like to do IVF again but I will do it for Kenny.

March 26, 2017

Round 3 IVF failed. We made it to embryo transfer, even having 2 "beautiful" embryos put in. The third embryo died in the lab. I am exhausted. I am physically and emotionally spent. That is the last time. I will have to find you another way.

August 9, 2017

We just got the email from Hausman and Hickman that a birth mother in Florida has chosen us to be your parents. You found us. We are on our way to meet the woman who is giving me the gift of motherhood.

November 17, 2017

We are on our way to Daytona to wait for your birth. We cannot wait to meet you.

Samantha was born at 6:38pm on November 29th. I was there in the room when she was born, witnessing an absolute miracle. I am forever humbled and grateful to Samantha's birth mother-my hero. She let me cut the umbilical cord and the doctors handed her to me.

2022

I am crying as I write this remembering the intense emotions of those days in the hospital, falling in love, waiting, signing legal papers, sitting with strangers, hearing other mothers, the amazing nurses who taught me how to feed her........The experience we had gave me so much respect for all women and all moms.

CHAPTER 3
Amanda

Y ou know those women who have always known they want to be a mom? The little girls that love to play with their baby dolls, the ones who love to babysit as teens, the ones who grow into the women who long for babies of their own and their chance to raise a family? The women who are meant to be moms? I was never one of those.

I never wanted kids; at least that's what I thought for a very long time. Ask my family and friends and they will tell you I always said, with conviction, "I don't want kids!" So what did I want? I wanted horses, dogs, medical school, a career, and maybe a husband if one happened to come along. I was young and busy, with a full life and a love of independence. Kids didn't fit into the picture I had of my life.

All of that changed when I met my husband Mike at a bar in Boston on New Year's Eve during my final year of pharmacy school. My plans to graduate and go on to medical school turned into an engagement and plans for a wedding. Mike and I soon had nieces and nephews that we adored and I thought, "I want this."

· · ·

Whoa. I wanted a baby?

For our one-year anniversary Mike and I took a trip to Punta Cana. We had been casually trying to conceive for four months at that time and over dinner and plenty of drinks (it was all inclusive so, "when in Rome") we started talking about babies. I was surprised that we hadn't seen those two pink lines and I was beginning to worry. After all, we were both young and healthy and it seemed to happen so quickly to everyone else we knew! I mentioned my worries and although he wasn't worried, he understood. We talked about it and decided that if six months went by and there was still no baby that I would start to think about going back to school instead of continuing to try for a baby; that had been my plan anyway and maybe that is what I was meant to do. So after a few more months of negative pregnancy tests I decided to take the GRE and start applying to Physician Assistant programs.

What a waste of time and money that study prep and GRE turned out to be; we found out we were pregnant the next month.

After months of trying for a baby and finding out there was in fact a baby we both had feelings of shock, excitement, disbelief, and happiness. There was much more happiness after our first ultrasound and genetic testing results confirmed our baby was a healthy boy. I started reading all the books I could on pregnancy and babies, I downloaded all the baby name apps and pregnancy apps, I signed Mike and I up for labor and childcare classes at the hospital, I ate all the right foods, I exercised and stayed active; I was going to start this whole Mom thing off on the right foot. What I lacked in experience I hoped to make up for in preparation and knowledge.

My pregnancy was fantastic and easy compared to some of the stories I heard from other moms. I felt lucky that I felt good and was amazed at what my body was capable of – I was growing a human! Those last two weeks though? They were tough. Our son was born in September 2016 and it was hot. It was the hottest summer in the history of summers if you asked me. By the time those final weeks rolled around I felt huge, and I was done. Thankfully, our baby was also done and decided to make his appearance almost two weeks early. Since it was nearly two weeks before our due date I had a hard time believing I was really in labor. "First babies are always late," everyone told me.

Not our Andrew! My labor was intense and fast and I wish someone had informed me about back labor (had to Google that one). I had planned on laboring at home as long as I could, and also didn't want to get sent home from the hospital like so many first-time moms do, so by the time we got to the hospital a few hours later my contractions were three minutes apart and I was already 8cm dilated. The nurses couldn't believe it and neither could I. We were whisked up to the Labor and Delivery floor right away and our beautiful boy was born a short while later. "Are you sure this is your first baby?" one nurse asked. "You were made for this! If you have any more babies you better camp out in the parking lot!" said another nurse.

When they placed our son on my chest I was in awe. I was elated! Exhausted, but elated. Little did I know the roller-coaster I had just gotten on. When you are pregnant everyone tells you about the joys of motherhood and how amazing those newborn days are, but not many tell you about the challenges or how truly hard it can become. Sure, they tell you that you'll lose a lot of sleep but it usually ends there. Very quickly

I began to think that becoming a mom was the hardest thing I had ever done and I wished someone had told me that is how it can be.

Andrew was beautiful and perfect; just as I had imagined him to be my entire pregnancy. But Mike and I were first-time parents and horribly inexperienced; we didn't know something was wrong. Our baby cried, oh he cried! It seemed like he never slept. Aren't babies supposed to sleep?

In those first few days we were home from the hospital I waited for the moment I had pictured during my pregnancy - that moment when Andrew and I looked into each other's eyes and bonded and felt that unconditional love that you hear about; but that moment didn't come. Instead, I felt as though everything was an impossible chore that I couldn't handle. I felt exhausted, overwhelmed, crushing sadness and near constant tears, a fear of leaving the house, and resentment towards this tiny human I was completely responsible for. I mourned my old life and my freedom; how could I have taken it for granted? I couldn't fathom a time when I had thought I wanted this, because "this" turned out to be a baby who cried almost constantly that I couldn't console and a life I no longer recognized, or wanted. I couldn't understand why anyone would want "this" because it was all so terrible.

Andrew would wake up every 45 minutes at night - so frequently that I couldn't fall asleep in between his wake ups and would be awake for hours. He would wake up screaming and nothing I, or my husband, tried seem to soothe him for long. I would stay up for hours, anxiously Googling tips and tricks for colicky babies, to no avail. When it became too much our closest friends would offer to take care of him overnight and we were so desperate that a few times we took them up on that offer just to get some sleep.

During the day I would count the hours from when my husband went to work until he came home. There were days that I looked at the clock to see it was past lunch and I hadn't had anything to eat or drink, hadn't yet washed my face or brushed my teeth, hadn't changed out of my spit up covered clothes because Andrew couldn't be put down. I spent all day trying to soothe him, to get him to stop crying, to get him to sleep but it was impossible. Some days I put him in his swing, wailing but safe, and brought food outside to eat on the patio alone because I needed to eat and couldn't listen to him anymore. Most days I cried just as much as he did. As dinner-time drew near anxiety would set in as I dreaded another sleepless night.

I was exhausted and felt utterly defeated and helpless. Wasn't I "made for this?" I started to think that maybe my family would be better off without me; maybe I wasn't meant to do this after all. Some days I thought it would be better for everyone if I just packed a bag, got in the car, and drove away.

I vividly remember sitting down to fill out the postpartum depression questionnaire at my six-week postpartum visit. There was no way I could possibly answer the questions honestly. I didn't even want to admit to myself or my family how I was feeling and the thoughts I was having, so how was I going to admit it to a stranger? What would they do if they knew how I was feeling? Surely they would think I was a terrible person, an unfit mother, and take my baby away. While waiting for the doctor I sat and stared at those questions and I cried. I cried and then I lied. When the doctor came in I handed him the questionnaire, answered all of his questions with answers I thought he wanted to hear, and then got in my car and drove home even though it was the last place in the world I wanted to be.

My mom always said I was a difficult baby that had terrible colic but Andrew, she said, was so much worse than I was. When I was in labor I called her to let her know and since she is a flight attendant she was able to catch the next flight up and even arranged her schedule so that she was able to spend two weeks with us. I tried to tell her that Mike and I would be all right and wanted that time to bond with Andrew but I am thankful she didn't listen because they were rough weeks. She would stay up with us and help try to soothe Andrew. She changed diapers and held my screaming child so I could go to the bathroom or shower or eat. She helped with our dogs, cleaned our house, and held my hand while I cried and couldn't stop. At the end of those first two weeks I begged her to take Andrew with her back to Florida as I drove her to the airport. Once she was out of the car and in the airport terminal I pulled over and just sobbed.

After those two weeks my mom came up to stay with us nearly every other week. Later on, she admitted it was more to take care of me than to take care of Andrew; she was afraid for me and worried that every time she left to go home it would be the last time she saw me. When Andrew was nearly three months old my mom looked at me and said, "I'm not leaving until you call your doctor. Something isn't right. You're not you." That morning I called my OB/GYN office and told them, through tears, how I was feeling. The medical assistant put me on hold for a few minutes and when she got back on the line asked if I could come into the office as soon as possible.

When the doctor came into the exam room and we started talking I couldn't stop crying. I was ashamed, embarrassed, and afraid to admit how I had been feeling and the kind of thoughts I had been having. The doctor picked up Andrew, carried my diaper bag, and led me to his office where we could sit and talk. He was calm and compassionate and let me cry and talk until I was done. He understood what I was feeling and told me he thought I had severe postpartum depression and anxiety. He didn't make me feel ashamed or guilty and he didn't make me feel like I was any less of a mother. That day we made a plan for me to see a therapist and start medication; he introduced me to resources I didn't know existed that helped other moms who felt the way I did. Although it took me a few weeks to begin to feel better, that day was a turning point for my family and I. Although Andrew was still difficult, I started to feel as though I could actually handle it. Medication and therapy helped me process my feelings and gave me the tools I needed to care for my family and myself.

Even though I was changing and feeling better, Andrew still wasn't. He was still inconsolable, rarely slept, cried all of the time, was gassy, and we began noticing changes in his stool. I spoke with other moms and researched Andrew's symptoms. I started keeping track of what I was eating and how Andrew was after I nursed him. I began to be concerned about food sensitivities based on what I was reading and seeing in him. Despite seeing our pediatrician several times about my concerns with Andrew they insisted it was simply colic, that he would outgrow it, and it was normal to be concerned since I was a first-time mom. The doctor reasoned that since Andrew was gaining weight that everything must be fine but I could try to eliminate dairy from my diet to see how Andrew responded.

After weeks of eliminating dairy with little improvement in Andrew I began to get frustrated. Not only was Andrew not feeling better, but I was starting to feel worse. I felt hungry all the time, was losing weight quickly, and having a hard time with my new dairy-free diet. Our pediatrician recommended I eliminate soy from my diet as well and finally agreed to refer us to a pediatric gastroenterologist. Over the next week my diet was even more limited than it had been before and one morning, while pumping, I passed out on the kitchen floor – my blood sugar had dropped so low. When we finally met with the gastroenterologist they confirmed what I had suspected; Andrew had a cow's milk protein allergy and soy intolerance.

Due to my rapid weight loss, difficulty with the dietary restrictions Andrew needed, and episode of passing out the doctor recommended we stop breastfeeding and start a special formula that Andrew would be better able to tolerate. Even though in my heart I knew this would be best for Andrew I was devastated; wasn't breastfeeding best for Andrew? How could I bond with my child, with whom I already had had a hard time bonding with, if I could no longer breastfeed?

After a lot of thought and a long talk with my husband we decided to transition Andrew to formula. How could I take care of Andrew if I couldn't eat what I needed to and was passing out? I needed to take care of myself if I wanted to be able to take care of Andrew too.

Like everything else had been with Andrew, the transition to formula and bottles was another obstacle. He didn't seem to want to take any of the five bottles we tried and he certainly didn't want to take a bottle from me. At each feeding I would hold my hungry, screaming baby and cry right along with him when he refused the bottle and rooted at my chest; it broke my heart. To add insult to injury, it took many uncomfortable weeks for my milk to finally dry up. But with time my milk dried up, we found a bottle that Andrew would take (even from me!), and I began to feel an unexpected sense of relief that I was no longer solely responsible for feeding our son. My husband was able to feed him just as readily as I and we even began to split overnight duties since Andrew was still waking frequently at night. For months I slept in our guest bedroom from 8pm until 1am while my husband was on night duty and then at 1am we would swap; I didn't think we would ever sleep in the same bed again.

Finally, when Andrew was 5 months old we began to see a change. By that time I had gotten a handle on my postpartum depression and anxiety and felt as though I was finally bonding with my son. I was able to look at him and feel love instead of resentment, and although I felt like I had to make up for those first few months I missed out on, I was starting to enjoy motherhood. Around that time Andrew had also been on formula for a few weeks and the milk proteins and soy had worked their way out of his system and he seemed to finally feel better! Our days and nights saw more smiles and sleep and less crying for the first time. We were finding our rhythm (with the help of some gentle sleep training)!

My husband and I adored Andrew – he was so much fun to be around and we were really starting to see his sweet personality for what felt like the first time. Just as we turned a corner though, the questions started: When are you having another? Doesn't he need a sibling? Don't you want another baby?

In my mind, the answer to these questions was "Never! No! Definitely not!"

Between my emotional health and Andrew's physical health we had had such a difficult time for five months. There were times our marriage felt strained, we were both almost always exhausted, and our lives felt like they had been flipped upside down for months. Things had just gotten better for us as a family. Why rock the boat?

When friends or family, and people in general, ask when you are having another baby and you tell them you think you might not have another baby it is generally not met with a positive response. You get a great deal of unsolicited advice on the dangers of only children and how lonely your child will be as an only child. "Who will Andrew have when you are gone?" Yikes – that's a lot to think about at the ripe old age of 29 with an infant! It was hard to explain the reasons we did not want another baby but Mike and I agreed that our family was in a good place, just the three of us.

The older Andrew got, the easier things seemed to get. After nearly seven months Andrew was sleeping through the night, which meant Mike and I were also sleeping through the night (and no one was sleeping in the guest room!). We had a routine and our son was the sweetest, most amazing child I could have ever asked for. I was able to find the joy in motherhood; something I didn't think I ever would have ever been able to do. Before either Mike or I knew it, we were celebrating Andrew's third birthday. Our smart, sweet, affectionate boy was three! He was incredible and we loved him more than anything. Our lives had a rhythm and a routine and most of the time, our days felt easy – something I never imagined would have ever happened. But something else I never imagined would happen started to happen; Andrew began to realize that other kids had brothers and sisters and occasionally he would ask for a baby. At first, Mike and I would laugh and tell him that maybe someday he would get a baby but then we started to consider it. Hey – that newborn phase doesn't last forever, right? Most days it seemed like a distant memory. A bad memory, but a distant one.

Fast-forward five months later, almost four years to the day we found out we were pregnant with Andrew, I was holding a positive home pregnancy test! I was happy and terrified all at the same time – were we really going to do this again? Were we crazy?! It didn't feel real but I called my doctor's office to make our first ultrasound appointment. We slowly started telling our immediate family and closest friends. What was the harm in sharing our exciting news? We had already had a healthy pregnancy and child.

The morning of our first ultrasound my mom, husband, and I drove to the office. We were in our ninth week and despite all the pregnancy symptoms I had been feeling I was still excited to see our baby. On the screen, the doctor showed us our tiny baby but we did not see a heartbeat; I knew immediately something was not right. The doctor encouraged us not to worry because our dates could simply be off and we weren't as far along as we thought. Before leaving we were scheduled for another ultrasound appointment the following week. My mom and husband were hopeful and positive but all I felt was a sinking feeling; I knew our dates couldn't be that far off.

One week later at our second ultrasound appointment the sinking feeling I had felt for the last week was confirmed. We had lost our baby.

A "missed miscarriage" the doctor called it. Our baby was gone but my body didn't know it; my pregnancy symptoms had continued even though the pregnancy had not. How could my body have missed that? My constant fatigue, swollen breasts, bloated belly, and nausea felt like a slap in the face.

Another week went by and I was scheduled for surgery because I wasn't naturally miscarrying. That morning my husband and I sat in pre-op for what felt like hours. The couple on the other side of the curtain, just feet from where I lay on the gurney, was waiting to be taken to the operating room for a scheduled C-section. We could hear their doctor and nurses congratulate them each time they went in to check on them. I hoped they couldn't hear our care team give us their condolences. At the time it seemed cruel to be placed next to these happy, expectant parents. I will never forget that cold morning in February when I walked into the hospital carrying our baby and walked out a few hours later without our baby.

That afternoon I went home to rest with a pamphlet and heavy pads and returned to work the following day. Just one week later the Covid-19 pandemic started. I imagine our miscarriage would have felt lonely and isolating even if I had been surrounded by people, but being physically isolated from others made my island of grief feel even more remote. I threw myself into work to occupy my mind and time. For weeks I worked 60+ hours per week and picked up as many shifts as I could at the hospital I worked at. My work gave me a sense of purpose during a time when I felt I had failed.

Time marched on and spring turned into summer. The pandemic continued and our family of three made the most of it and enjoyed our time home together. My husband and I grieved our loss but continued to enjoy our son. At first, I felt convinced that maybe we were meant to be "one and done" as we had previously thought. But in time my feelings changed and so did my husband's. We started to warm up to the idea of trying again.

On my birthday in July, while on a family vacation, I took a pregnancy test and was shocked to see those two pink lines. Cautiously optimistic would best describe our feelings this time around. Knowing how difficult it can be to tell people about a pregnancy loss after you've shared your pregnancy news with them, we kept our news quiet.

The morning of our first ultrasound appointment was full of mixed feelings; apprehension, excitement, fear. Due to Covid precautions my husband was unable to come with me to this appointment, or any of our prenatal appointments, and that added to my fear and apprehension. If we got bad news at an appointment, I would have to hear it alone.

Our first ultrasound showed a perfect tiny baby with a strong heartbeat. I couldn't hold back tears of relief. I walked out of the appointment to my husband waiting in the car and showed him the ultrasound pictures. Each of our early appointments would follow this pattern, but my optimism remained cautious at best. Even with my horrendous all day "morning sickness," our positive genetic testing results, having heard and seen a strong heartbeat our experience of having had a missed miscarriage reminded me that we could lose this baby and not even know it.

I felt some relief as I started to feel our baby moving. Those movements, even the early ones, gave me reassurance each time that our baby was okay. Despite this small sense of relief I was still hesitant to announce our pregnancy even though my belly was starting to give it away. After our 20-week anatomy scan I finally felt confident sharing the news that we were expecting a baby girl! Although the remainder of our pregnancy went by without any issues, the fear of losing our baby never completely went away. Being pregnant after a prior loss is scary and it is difficult to be positive sometimes. What added to my fear was the possibility of developing postpartum depression and anxiety a second time. Would it happen again? Would it be worse? Could I really go through that again? I certainly didn't want our son to see me like that.

My husband and son helped me stay positive; their happiness and excitement was infectious. Mike was so excited to have a daughter, especially since Andrew has always been a "mama's boy." Andrew couldn't wait to be a big brother and was so excited to have a baby sister. He would, and still does, refer to her as his baby.

One week before our due date I bent down to help Andrew with his socks and my water broke. Our Nora was ready to go! Later that evening, after another fast and intense labor and delivery, our baby girl was safely with us! Every moment of fear and apprehension was worth seeing her sweet face and holding her in my arms. Looking her I couldn't believe we had ever thought that we were "one and done."

In the days that followed I was hyper-aware of my every emotion. My husband, family, friends, and I knew that I was more likely to develop postpartum depression and anxiety again. Through being vocal about my prior postpartum struggles my family and friends knew the signs and knew what to watch for. Every day at least one person would ask how I was feeling, how I was doing, and if I needed anything. Each morning I woke up waiting to feel what I had felt in the days that followed Andrew's birth. I was afraid to tell people we were doing well for fear I would jinx it. I felt like I was waiting for the other shoe to drop.

Today Nora is two months old. She is a wonderful baby, though I think any baby would feel like a walk in the park after Andrew. She is happy almost all of the time and I can't help but feel love when I look at her. We recognized and realized, in the first two weeks, that Nora has severe reflux and a cow's milk protein allergy just like her brother had. This time around though we were persistent and advocated for her to her pediatrician. This time around giving up dairy for her hasn't been the impossible obstacle it felt like last time I had to do it while nursing Andrew. This time around I know this phase isn't forever and I am prepared to deal with it. This, I know now, is what it should be like.

Not every woman's journey to motherhood is as beautiful as they imagine it will be. Pregnancy isn't all glowing skin and beautiful hair; sometimes its morning sickness and anxiety. The newborn phase isn't always an easy and beautiful breast-feeding journey that creates an amazing bond between mother and child; sometimes its painful, hard, overwhelming, and discouraging. Not every woman's body goes back to what it once was; sometimes your skin is a little stretched and your hips are a little wider.

You give up your body for the better part of a year to nourish and grow a healthy child. You persevere through the pain of labor and delivery to safely bring your child into this world. Your life changes in every imaginable way once your child arrives and your first job is to care for them, even while your body is healing. You sacrifice your body, your time, your freedom, your sleep, and so much more. Some days it feels like you have given up everything for this little person, but other days it feels like this little person has given you everything.

From their first smiles and words to their laughter and love, our children bring light and happiness to our lives. Their unconditional love heals us even when we didn't know we needed it. They forgive us when we lose our tempers, they tell jokes when we need to smile, and they still reach for us at the end of the day (even the bad ones).

I may not have been meant to be a mother, but I was made to be Andrew and Nora's mom.

CHAPTER 4

Meg

I had always pictured myself as a mother of many children. I came from a large family, my sister had a large family, and I desperately wanted a large family of my own to care for and love.

I got pregnant with my first son fairly easily, I don't think I was off birth control for even three months. I had what I know now was an early miscarriage before getting pregnant with Dylan. Things just weren't "right" with what I had initially chalked up as a late period. Those around me told me it wasn't a big deal and that there was absolutely nothing I could do about it, so just let "nature take its course". My pregnancy with my first son was considered high-risk because I couldn't gain weight, my blood pressure was alarmingly high, and I was under an enormous amount of stress. I was put on bed rest for almost my entire last trimester, but even that proved to be stressful because I didn't have a very good support system and I was often told I was being "lazy" and that I was using my pregnancy as an excuse to not be active, despite the doctor's strict orders. My labor and delivery were fast and hard, I had been discouraged from attending any sort of childbirth class, so I just sort of learned as I went along. I was terrified because an ultrasound had shown that the umbilical cord was wrapped around the baby's neck. My doctor was amazing, though, and we welcomed Dylan Jack into the world, a healthy and wonderful baby boy.

When Dylan was just a few months old, I discovered I was pregnant again. My body wasn't happy to be pregnant and once more I had a very difficult time gaining weight, controlling my blood pressure, and I was sick often. With a little one to care for and working at a law office and owning my own business, it was impossible for me to go on bed rest as once again ordered, and I just kept going at 100% all the time. While continuing to be at full speed worked great for those around me, it was a mistake for me to do this. Shane was born a few weeks early with complications and I struggled greatly with my own recovery. What was worse, after I returned home from the hospital, I painfully passed a large mass and bled heavily. My heart rate and blood pressure were out of control, and I fainted at one point. This was not normal. My doctor told me that it was likely an undeveloped twin that my body naturally expelled after giving birth to Shane. I was devastated but was told that "this was just nature's way" and to just focus on and be grateful for my healthy children.

Fast forward another few months, I was pregnant again. I was, admittedly, overwhelmed. I had two little boys already who needed me, and I was afraid I wouldn't be able to handle a third child. However, I quickly fell in love with the baby I was carrying and was certain it was going to be another boy. My mom and I picked the name "Rand Cole" and we started to make lots of plans for me to be a mama of three. Unfortunately, I miscarried Rand. It was painful, it was traumatic, and I was told by everyone around me that I was foolish to grieve. One tactless person referred to it as "God's way of weeding out the runts." Wow. I guess my baby was a runt, something easily lost and cast aside.

I went to the doctor twice for this miscarriage. Once, to an emergency room. I was with some extended family members out of state when I started to bleed. It cut our visit short because I needed to be seen at an ER. Hurtful comments made to me, such as, "Everyone bleeds during pregnancy, you're being dramatic" and the worst of all, during my time at the ER, someone said, "Well, I guess we're going to have to make this trip to see family every weekend until you can get it right." The next day, it was apparent that my condition was deteriorating. I arranged for childcare for my two sons and drove myself to the clinic. There, I fully miscarried. In the examination room, a doctor said to me, "You probably have STDs, that is the main reason anyone would bleed while pregnant." I assured him that I had no sexually transmitted diseases and felt I was miscarrying my child. When two interns put on headband-style lights to examine me, they remarked to one another that they looked like Native Americans and proceeded to make very racist jokes, laughing loudly as I cried. Then, they told me I had "spontaneously aborted" and left the room. I was so alone. There was blood everywhere. I was given nothing to clean up with. I was in such a daze, I just used the small sink in the exam room and rough paper towels, along with the white paper sheet from the examination table to do my best to clean up. I also felt guilty and was embarrassed that the room was such a mess with my blood that I also did my best to clean the room, too. No one came back into the room, so I just finally left. I was weak, disoriented, and in shock. I then waited two hours for my ride, who was very irritated that I couldn't just pull it together and drive myself home. The ride home was in complete silence except for the pounding of my broken heart.

They say that healing begins when you bear witness. That

miscarriage occurred 23 years ago, and I have never told anyone the truth about what happened to me and the trauma that was inflicted upon me by uncaring medical professionals, the ignorance of those around me, and the deep shame I felt that I had lost my child in such a demeaning way. I was taught to not make waves, to stay quiet when people hurt me, and that miscarrying a child was not something to be talked about. Today, with this writing, and in sharing my story, I finally bear witness. I finally am telling my truth, and I pray that by telling it, someone else might feel that they are not alone. Perhaps now I will heal.

CHAPTER 5

Kristi

F or my daughter, Maggie.

Maggie,

If I can teach you anything, I hope I can teach you the importance of giving up. In the many years we tried to bring your spirit earth-side, I didn't give up once. I gave up dozens of times.

The important thing to remember about giving up is to always begin again. And so I did, year after year, doctor after doctor, push after push.

While I never lost sight of you, giving up allowed me to curate the world I welcomed you to. And I wouldn't trade the journey for anything.

Love, Mum

I'm convinced it was mind over matter. After a lifetime of being told that I was a miracle baby, after my parents suffered a decade of heartbreak before conceiving me, I think I made myself believe I would struggle to conceive, too. So when I did, with no medical reason behind it, it made sense. And sometimes that would bring me comfort and it would hurt less, but it always hurt.

I gave up. I pushed those feelings down and threw myself into work, growing a small company into a recognized name in the industry it served. As the company grew, so did my responsibilities. I could and would do it all. Further efforts in conceiving a child became more of an afterthought. How could I do both? I chose business over baby, as many do. I babied the hell out of the company. It became my livelihood, my family, everything. I felt like I'd achieved what I pined for: a sense of motherhood. My heart ached knowing full well this feeling was just a sense, a placeholder.

So, I gave up the notion that it had to be one or the other and set off to balance both dedication to my work and fighting to fill the space saved in my heart for a baby. Making every effort to succeed at work and growing a family, this looked like doctor appointments at the break of dawn and scheduling treatments that would not conflict with company events. I believed I had been making motherhood the priority, but looking back it was clear which baby I was nurturing. It became increasingly harder to juggle both. With business booming and treatments failing new levels of exhaustion were achieved. I couldn't do it all.

So I gave up. I asked for help, delegated down, and I started being selfish (to read: started taking care of myself). For the first time in over half a decade of trying, I made myself the priority. I went to acupuncture, practiced self-care, joined a support group for women with fertility issues. I realized that I didn't have to say yes to everything to feel successful and didn't have to stay busy to feel the same. I healed a wound I didn't know existed and re-introduced myself to... me.

It wasn't happenstance that I had found the balance I'd

always struggled to attain. I needed to give up to set boundaries and to learn patience. I needed to give up to learn that it was okay to want and ask for help. I didn't need all these tools to be the mom my baby needed but the mom I wanted to be. But it was after all this that she appeared.

Giving up didn't mean failure. It meant finding ways to make me whole.

CHAPTER 6

Griffen

My journey all started when I was just a kid, a girl in the sixth grade fresh with life. I'll never forget the horrible pain I was in and going to the hospital 3 times over a one-week span. Doctor after doctor couldn't explain what was happening. One told me it was gas and to go home, another sent me home with opioids for the pain and told me to just rest. But it wasn't until my whole body went stiff and I couldn't move that action was taken. I had to call the mom of the kids I was babysitting for to take me home ASAP, as something was terribly wrong. Turned out I was getting blood poisoning from the dead ovary and fallopian tubes that had been causing me such pain. I had surgery right away.

So, I lived with knowing it would be a little hard for me to have children. As a little girl at the time, I didn't understand or cared that much.

As time went on, I developed two types of endometriosis causing more pain, and in the long run contributing to my infertility.

Flash forward to right after my husband and I were

married. Immediately wanting to start our family, we went to the best of the best infertility doctor in our area. I remember meeting with him and doing all of our tests before going ahead with IVF. Everything was perfect! Test results were amazing, and I was most certain that we had this in the bag.

Boy was I wrong! A month of driving back and forth over an hour each way to get to the doctor before 7 a.m. for blood work, ultrasounds, talks with the nurses...a month of hope and waiting. A month of pumping myself full of hormones, shots in my butt, shots in my belly. But after our first egg retrieval we got awful news. I was groggy, still coming out of the anesthesia but I remember being so excited to see how many eggs were recovered. None...we got not one healthy, viable egg. With having one ovary that was supposed to be so healthy and functional, little did we know that there was more to the story. I was devastated. After a week to recoup, we went back and had a meeting with our doctor. He wasn't confident as he told me that my condition would require me going to another country to fix the abnormalities. He said we could give it another go but to start looking into egg donor options.

I left feeling defeated as my husband tried to console me. Together we felt gutted and didn't know what to do. Perhaps we should consider an egg donor. Perhaps we should consider adoption, a process I was totally comfortable with having myself been adopted by the most amazing parents and I knew I would be able to pay that love forward. There was just so much to consider that my head was spinning.

After a few weeks of having my pity party I decided I wasn't going to take no for an answer. I knew there was something I could do and I was going to find every damn answer I could. The research began, the books being read were piled high, article after article completed. But I was beginning to find something and holy shit, it felt good.

We decided to go for another round. This time I was

going to space it out, allowing everything I was starting to do for myself- the supplements, the natural remedies- to reach their full effect so I could get so called "healthy" eggs. It was indeed a whole lifestyle change but I was willing to start my fight and fight hard.

Second IVF round. We got closer... We got one mediocre egg. This one gave me hell. The waiting game was intense, and I just remember sitting at my counter with my phone in front of me, trying but not succeeding in keeping it all together, I couldn't breathe, and I couldn't stop crying. I didn't know what the doctor was going to say. It was day 6 so it was either now or freeze it for a future transfer day.

I got the call, the decision was made to freeze it and we would start the whole frozen embryo transfer process. If you have ever done this, you will know that the drugs are more intense and can easily turn even an angel into Satan. Man, did I hate that month of torture!

It was Mother's Day, and I had the embryo implanted. We were living in a camper at the time, and although the living conditions weren't the best, we were getting by day by day.

That next week we went for blood work to see if I was pregnant, and it was a hard no.

The doctor said it would never happen for us and that if we wanted to work with him again we would need to find a donor.

Defeated once again, and this time at only 27 and the healthiest I had ever been in my entire life. But something grew stronger in me, and I knew for a fact that defeat wasn't going to be the thing that defined me. I knew I was going to be a mother even if I had to get a little creative. I just needed time.

I continued my health journey for the next two years. We were out of money to pay for IVF again so we spent what we did have, time, on being "us". We were a family already, just my husband and I. Although we were content, we both knew what we longed for and we weren't ready to just give up.

When the time was right, we went to another doctor. Finally, someone new with a new perspective. Now we were excited! We started the new process, same shots in the butt and tummy, blood work again and again. Egg extraction day came and we were both so nervous, as we've been through this song and dance before.

12 eggs were extracted and Holy Mother of Joseph, we had amazing eggs! Four ended up being top grade and we were able to do a fresh transfer with two. I always wanted twins so we just went for it.

After we went back for pregnancy blood work, we got the call I've always dreamed of. "You're pregnant!!"

Tears just ran down my face. Never in my life did I ever think that I would be able to hear those two amazing words. Words of hope and words for a future.

The blood work also came back super high, so guess what? Twins!

A couple weeks went by, and I was just living on cloud nine. Being super careful with everything I did (after all this was my first pregnancy and it only took three years). I would hardly move; I was that girl who thought if I did anything they would simply slip out!

We went back in for blood work and ultrasound, but it wasn't the news I had hoped for. They said my blood levels had dropped tremendously and that we could just be losing one baby. They said to come back in in two days for a recheck.

I remember I was at a job the next day, staging a home. I went to the bathroom and my nightmare was coming to life. The life that was once with me was now gone.

Showing up to the doctor's office was brutal. I couldn't

keep it together as the nurses tried to hug me. They too were in tears.

We decided to wait and let my body heal before we went through with another frozen cycle.

But guess what? I was able to get pregnant! Something I was told would never happen for me. Pregnant, and with my own eggs! I had done it against all odds.

On the next frozen transfer day we decided again, to implant two eggs. We had nothing left to lose. This was my last and final attempt. I couldn't put myself or my husband through this again.

It's a girl!

My heart and soul had never been better, never been happier. This was happening. We did it.

But it did not come easily even after all we had been through.

I was a lunch with my husband, and I went to the bathroom. There was blood everywhere and I started to panic. I couldn't breathe. No no no, not again. Not this far in, no! I ran out to my husband, and I screamed I'm going to the ER, I think I'm losing Joey.

5 hours waiting. 5 of the worst hours of my life just waiting to get an answer.

Baby is fine! Apparently, my body wasn't healed after all from the miscarriage and it caused bleeding and a huge clot.

I was put on bed rest and I bled for 6 months. Everyday and every time I bled I thought I was losing my girl. It was so unsettling. My OB was so amazing and I went in to see him every week. We had an ultrasound every week so I could have peace of mind that my girl was going to be OK.

Nine months in and we had lost my mother-in-law from lung cancer. It was one of the hardest things to go through as I watched my husband mourn while we were trying to be excited for our girl to arrive. My poor body had had enough after planning the funeral and reception. No sleep, on my feet nonstop but I had to do this. I knew my mother-in-law was watching over our girl and nothing would happen to her.

I opted for being induced a week early. Something was telling me that this was the right decision. I just wanted my girl and I wanted her to be out as we had worked so hard for this.

I labored for 23 hours and the time came for a C-section.

When they delivered herI felt something wasn't right. I could barely hold her. I felt like I was dying. My heart rate dropped and a team rushed in to bring me back. Joey had to be out on oxygen at the same time and my husband ,who had just lost his mom, was watching helplessly the whole time. He ran down the hall as he couldn't take this again.

We were OK!

The doctor came in and told us we had made the right choice to be induced when we did. There were two infections that we were not aware of. If we had waited for full term, Joey would have been dead.

Someone was watching out for us all after all.

Joey girl is now four years old and is the light of our lives. She will be our one and only but that one and only was meant for us. She was the one that we worked so hard for. She is the reason whyI advocate to NEVER give up on something that means so much to you. She is my why.

CHAPTER 7

Min

July 24, 2014 will be a date I will never forget. This will be a date that is forever imprinted on my heart. We had to say goodbye to our first daughter, Yuna Hope. She was a fighter until her very last breath. She was our first born, she was our everything, and now she is our Angel baby.

Let me take you on a short journey before Yuna Hope. My husband and I had been trying for a couple of years to get pregnant. We were not expecting for our attempts to take so long. We were both young, healthy, active, and eager. We went to a friend's wedding in San Diego, CA and during the reception I broke out in bright red rashes. I had absolutely no clue as to what was happening to my body. Envision a human with red cheetah spots all over their body because that is what I looked like. I covered up in my husband's jacket and immediately left after the ceremony. We rushed to the ER and sure enough this was when we found out we were blessed with a baby. The rashes came from my sensitivity to cats and being pregnant just happened to heighten my sensitivities. Red splotches all over my body, but you could not damper my joy from the news of being pregnant! I was going to be a MOMMY!

At the time we resided in Monterey, CA where my husband Patrick was attending Naval Post Graduate School. We had to wait until I was about 10 weeks along before I could be seen by an OBGYN. I was nervous beyond measure for my appointment, but I was also excited to hear our baby's heartbeat. The initial appointment went wonderful. The heartbeat sounded strong and I was elated to have our pregnancy confirmed. I had minimal pregnancy symptoms and my morning sickness was very seldom. I felt I had the pregnancy glow. I could have blinded a room full of people with my glow; at least that is how I felt every single day waking up pregnant.

It wasn't until our second OBGYN appointment that I felt anything negative. Up until this point, I was the ecstatic mom-to-be strutting her pregnant self everywhere and anywhere. As I laid on the hospital bed with cold gel on my belly, I had anxiety rush through me. Our doctor informed us of a liquid sack developing behind our baby's neck and we were referred to specialists at San Francisco Women's Healthcare. Mind you, during this visit no words were really spoken by the ultrasound tech. I, of course asked questions but I was informed they could not provide answers and that a doctor would be the one to share the results. A couple of weeks go by and I am just filled with angst and fears. I prayed every chance I had. When we arrived at the hospital, I had a panic attack to the point of hyperventilating. When the ultrasound was performed again, we had two doctors inform us that our daughter most likely has a chromosomal abnormality and that they could schedule for termination while we were present.

Without hesitation I yelled at the doctors and informed them a termination would not be an option. I would keep our baby for as long as a heartbeat existed. Further tests were performed; less than a week later we were contacted by one of the doctors, who told us our baby had Turner's Syndrome. Turner's Syndrome is only diagnosed in females, so this is how we also learned we were having a girl. Patrick and I spoke with multiple specialists and counselors at the hospital to provide us with all the resources available. We left the room feeling defeated, but I also left feeling grateful I still had our baby girl in me.

We read everything we could on Turner's Syndrome, and we felt we were equipped to take care of our baby girl. We were ready to fight the fight; we were going to do whatever it took to grow our family. She was a fighter, and she gave us "hope" to hold on. We found it only fitting to give her the middle name "Hope". Hope is what she gave us in the time of hardship. My pregnancy was now considered high-risk, so I saw my OBGYN frequently. He was against abortion and early termination. I will forever remember our OBGYN saying to us, "I will support whatever decision you both make". He also shared that he believed a child that can feel love and find their own unique way to show their love, deserved a life to live, and I couldn't agree more, so we kept fighting.

I am now 20 weeks at this point, my belly is growing, my baby is growing, but so is her liquid filled sack. In fact, our follow-on appointment only showed her sack not only growing but spreading to other parts of her body. She had liquid filling in her limbs. During this appointment, I had to return to the San Francisco Women's Healthcare hospital to determine further options. Since Patrick was in US Navy he was often traveling and he was in a different state during the time of this important appointment, so I was so fortunate to have a co-worker with me for support. She definitely was a God send. This was such a difficult time for me; I did not want to hear anymore bad news. I was just praying for a miracle.

At this appointment the doctors identified issues with her

heart, that were under-developed, uncertain whether this was a direct cause of Turner's Syndrome. The doctor performing my echo-ultrasound that identified the additional heart challenges was also pregnant. I have to admit she had the pregnancy glow too. Something about her told me this was her first pregnancy. When she told me Yuna Hope would not have a chance to survive, I lost it. I asked her "mother to mother, what would you do?" It took a moment which felt like forever, and I recall her telling me that her profession would not allow her to use the word "in pain," but she could tell me that our baby was in great discomfort. Two days later, Patrick had to fly back to Monterey on emergency leave as I was in labor.

I was in labor for about 17 hours, I was trying so hard to deliver Yuna Hope naturally. I felt it was my duty to do all that I could to prevent further harm and pain, so I thought natural delivery was the best way. I felt like I failed...I just could not endure the pain any longer. Once I was given the epidural it was only a matter of a couple of hours that Yuna Hope was delivered. She was born without a heartbeat, but she was breathing. The only reason why she was breathing was because she was still connected to me while in the womb. I was providing her with oxygen.

We held her in our arms, in a precious garment handmade by a wonderful non-profit organization Helping Hands-Angel Gowns. While we held her, we said many prayers, shed so many heart wrenching tears, and gave her lots of kisses. I couldn't fathom feeling any negative emotions while holding her...I didn't want her to feel any negativity projecting from me or her dad before going up to Heaven.

I asked the nurse to take her as we were done with our goodbyes. I didn't know if I would honestly have the courage to ever let go of her if I didn't in that moment. I was infuriated, I was heartbroken, and I felt I would never ever be the same.

We met with a great organization that assisted with coordinating burial services for lost loved ones, something I never imagined I would experience in my life. We had Yuna Hope cremated and spread over the San Francisco Bay area; her daddy being in the Navy means wherever in the world he may be on a ship, our Yuna Hope would be right along side him, and maybe even swimming with dolphins! Yuna Hope was expected to be due on December 28th, which happens to also be my birthday. So now with each passing birthday we celebrate myself and Yuna Hope. To this day December 28th is a very bitter-sweet day for me. We also celebrate the July 24 every year, the day she left this world.

To be transparent, I fully blamed myself. I think many women would in a similar situation, but maybe not for the same source as my guilt. Let me rewind my story to a few years earlier, when I unfortunately experienced a sexual assault from a military doctor when I was deployed. That experience left me with extreme PTSD, depression, and anxiety. I hated and feared anything related to hospitals. I felt like my only option was the emergency room (ER.) I would always allow my health to get so bad that the ER was truly the only option. I would battle Patrick and other family members when I needed to seek medical attention.

The moment I got pregnant I immediately had anxiety knowing how many doctor appointments I would need but we had waited so long to get pregnant that I fought my fears. As you can imagine I blamed myself for my daughter's struggles and ultimate goodbye. If I didn't have PTSD, severe anxiety, and struggles with depression would she be here today? The "what if's" constantly ran through my mind. The day we lost her it took everything in me to want to continue my life. I hated hospitals and doctors even more after our loss. To help with my daily struggles I started counseling and working. I started to feel stronger mentally and physically.

We decided to try and expand our family again, when I felt mentally ready. A few years later we found out we were pregnant again, unfortunately we suffered a miscarriage. I do not know how far along I was with our second baby, I couldn't ask the doctor after my D&C. I didn't have the strength, I just knew in the moment I failed again. All of my hurt feelings and emotions rushed to the surface of losing Yuna Hope all over again.

I felt so lost in this world. I wanted nothing more than to be a mother and to see my husband as a father, and now we had not one but two angel babies. It was a tough road after our 2nd loss, but all I could ever think about was how much Yuna Hope had fought for us. How her fight allowed us to feel her presence with us longer, so if I accepted defeat, I would be giving up too fast. So I didn't give up, I kept thinking about Yuna. I am so happy we did not give up.

On December 12, 2018 our beautiful daughter Mila was born! Our rainbow baby and our gift from Yuna Hope was here to stay. The joy from her birth until this day in indescribable. Patrick was deployed so he was not present during her birth, but with the help of God's timing he was able to return home for a very short time to meet his baby girl. They were able to bond for a couple of days before he traveled back to his ship. In those couple of days, the bond the three of us created is one that is forever unbreakable. This bond is one that Yuna Hope gifted to us. Mila is our rainbow baby, and Yuna Hope was the "Hope" that led us to our beautiful rainbow. Then 14 months later, we were blessed again, this time with our son Jakob! This was entirely unplanned, but we've learned it is always and will always be God's timing.

Both my children know of their sister Yuna Hope. They see the pictures we have with her in our room and they know where Yuna Bear is located, a beautiful gift from her grandparents. They also know any time they see butterfly it is their sister, coming to say "hi" to us. The loss of our babies will always be a difficult memory, but I chose to embrace the NOW, and live stronger and happier for all my babies. I know happy faces is what our babies ultimately want from us.

I share my story, so you know you're not alone experiencing the unimaginable pain of losing a loved one. The struggles of trying to get pregnant are also a lot to handle, but again you're not alone. Your angel babies are forever with you, and no matter the type of loss, your baby will forever have a positive imprint in your heart. They made you a mom! No one can take that title away from you. Hold onto "Hope," and know you deserve happiness. Please learn from me and steer away from blaming yourself and know you have a community of women that is here to keep you standing when you feel weak. You have a community of mothers that is here to endure the emotions with you. You are never alone!

CHAPTER 8

Jane

Never in my life did I imagine that my journey into motherhood would begin with grief. Before I go on any further, I will say that my story has a happy ending. My daughter, N. Hope, was my hope after loss, my sweet rainbow baby. I would do it all over again just to be her mother.

[There are not many spaces where I feel encouraged to share my story about becoming the mother of an angel baby, as death is a topic that makes people uncomfortable, particularly when talking about miscarriage, stillbirth, or infant loss. I am incredibly thankful for this sacred space to share my story without judgment (none that I will know about anyway) or fear that I am making someone else feel uncomfortable with my story.]

The very first time I got pregnant, it was after a couple years of trying. My husband and I were thrilled. We had just established care at a fertility clinic and were considering IUI, but we got lucky. Well . . . so we thought. About 6 weeks after seeing the double pink lines, which happened to be on Election Day, 2016, I had an early miscarriage. I started bleeding as I stood in line to vote that morning and it just didn't stop. My doctor confirmed that I had a blighted ovum, which is when a fertilized egg attaches itself to the uterine wall, but the embryo does not develop. In other words, there was a gestational sac seen on ultrasound, but no embryo. Dreams of a baby were immediately crushed, but I tried to convince myself that I did not need to grieve a loss because technically a baby did not start forming yet. However, it did not stop me from grieving what could have been. That day, in general, was soul-crushing for me and my husband, so I just buried my feelings beneath the distraction of news alerts and collective grief of those that expected the first female President of the United States to be elected.

In any event, we were not going to let up on our dreams to become parents, so we tried again. In April 2017, I learned that I was pregnant again. We were so scared to tell anyone given how delicate and fleeting the last pregnancy was for us. I was a nervous wreck about making it to the "magical 12-week mark," or the point at which many couples choose to share their good news on social media platforms. We did not publicly share the news, but I was starting to feel more and more hopeful with each passing week after that point. We found out that we were having a boy. We envisioned ourselves as parents to a wonderful little boy – he already changed our lives.

We named him Leo and we fell in love with him before we ever met him. He was perfect. I had an easy and uncomplicated pregnancy until the home stretch. One day, during the 32nd week, I noticed that my baby was moving less. I immediately called the doctor's office and was told to come in for a non-stress test which monitors the baby's heart rate. I kept telling myself over and over again "I'm sure everything is okay. Just paranoid, but everything will be fine." I recalled the statistics on viability should the baby need to be born at 32 weeks (it was as high as 95%). Even if he were to come now, he would be in the NICU, but he would be alive, I told myself. The nurses (two different ones) could not detect a heartbeat on the stress test. They thought it was a positioning issue. I was then sent to the ultrasound room where the technician held her breath as she was pressing the transducer into various parts of my very large belly. Before I knew it, she said she was grabbing the doctor. There is not much of this day that I remember in great detail, but I will never forget this. The doctor, voice soft and quivering, begins to tell me, "I'm so sorry . . . ." I laid there, in complete shock, hoping that she was wrong, hoping that this was not my reality. All I recall saying was, "No . . . no . . . that can't be." My world came crashing down. I was in an ocean and was drowning. It was as if someone took my own life.

The next thing I know, I'm being walked across the street to the hospital to be induced into labor. I made a phone call to my husband who was on a business trip, giving him the most devastating news he could possibly hear. I was told that the induction would take a while so my husband would certainly make it back in time for the birth. The birth?! It was beyond my comprehension that I still had to go through the birthing process. I asked for them to put me to sleep and perform a cesarean, but that was not the preferred option, as a vaginal birth was deemed safer for the mother. So, I started the induction process, all alone with a nurse I have just met. She was holding my hand and letting me cry uncontrollably until my family was able to come see me. The induction process took three days and it was excruciating. My cervix was not ready to deliver a baby at 32 weeks; it was sealed shut, which is what the cervix is expected to do at that point. They did all sorts of things to get labor going. At that point, I did not care what they did to my body. It didn't feel like my own. I had already died in my mind. When it was time, I pushed and pushed, and with encouragement from my husband and mother beside me, I finally gave birth to a beautiful sleeping angel. Giving birth is such an incredible act. It is empowering, transformative, and just so intensely beautiful. But for me, it was also profoundly devastating. My husband and I held our son, who as wrapped up in a newborn blanket, and wept and wept. We had so much love for this child that we just met and so much sadness that felt impossible to process.

Leo would be 4 years old today and there isn't a day that goes by where he doesn't cross my mind. When I see 4 year-old boys, I wonder how life would have been like had he been given a chance. Would he have been interested in dinosaurs? What would his favorite ice-cream flavor be? Would he look more like mommy or daddy? There is a whole life with my son that I will never know.

As if losing my son wasn't bad enough, not knowing why was like pouring salt into an open wound. As I have been told by several doctors, it is scientifically impossible to completely understand what happened. I could not wrap my brain around that. I refused to accept "I don't know" as an answer. The best they could do was surmise that it could possibly have been a cord injury. The hospital also lost my placenta (of all placentas to lose), so we did not have that piece of the puzzle. Tests performed on both me and my son turned up normal and did not provide any answers. He was a perfect little baby boy and my body created a hazard for him – that was ultimately the answer I left myself with at the end of the day. I will never really know what happened. This, as you can imagine, caused a host of psychological issues for me. I became distrustful of my body and extremely hypochondriacal. I was convinced that I had some sort of undiagnosed/uncovered disease or illness that ultimately was to blame. At one point, I had over 20 vials of blood taken from me in one sitting to test for every single potential autoimmune disease known to man. All of the tests came up normal. Yet my brain kept searching even though my heart knew that I won't solve this mystery. I recognized this obsessive-compulsive behavior I had developed – trying to play doctor, getting lost in Google's black hole of information, and convincing myself that understanding the reason why would bring me closer to closure – and I sought out a mental health professional who specifically dealt with patients who suffered similar types of losses. Therapy was a Godsend for me. It was my first big step towards healing and finding hope after loss.

I also couldn't have survived without my village of supporters – family, friends, co-workers, and yes, some strangers that I randomly found myself connecting with because they've also experienced some sort of tragic loss and found hope afterwards. I also met other women who have experienced pregnancy loss and we shared our stories and our pain. We are all part of this horrible sorority – mothers of angel babies – but we found comfort in each other. They did not make me feel alone. Because despite all of the flowers, gifts, sympathetic words, and other wonderful gestures we received, there is something so incredibly lonely about grieving a child that you carried that no one else got to know. Motherhood at this point was characterized by unrelenting sadness, grief, and longing. But I was still determined to have the family that I had dreamed of having with my husband. In fact, the only thing that kept me forward-looking and hopeful was the possibility of having a successful pregnancy next time. However, we came face to face with more obstacles.

Hope (the Merriam-Webster definition): to cherish a desire with anticipation: to want something to happen or be true. She was born a little more than 2 years after we lost Leo, right before the COVID-19 pandemic shut down the world. And she saved me.

Motherhood does not begin when you give birth. It starts much earlier. The pain that you go through to become a mother is very much a part of the unique journey that is yours. For better or for worse, it makes an imprint on your heart forever. My journey to becoming Hope's mother began with Leo. Without Leo, there would not be Hope.

When it became difficult to conceive again naturally, we gave it about six months before bringing in the big guns: IVF. We are very fortunate to be able to prioritize our resources to make this a possibility. Given all that we have gone through, it was taking an emotional toll on me to get that negative test result each month. Also, being in my late 30s at the time, I felt that time was my enemy. I did not want to be in the territory of statistics that showed less favorable outcomes. Given this pressure, we felt that IVF was the right choice for us, and we put all our trust (and money) into the fertility doctors we chose.

The IVF process felt long, drawn out, and frankly, remains a blur to this day. There were many medications, many needles, and timing and dosage had to be accurate. I am not sure how they trust us non-medical folks with this stuff, but it's certainly a leap of faith. I never thought that I'd be come an expert at administering subcutaneous injections into my abdomen. In any event, it was painstaking. I had to undergo the egg retrieval process twice (and of course all the medication protocol leading up to it) because after embryo testing, I had no healthy embryos from the first round. The second time around, I got several healthy embryos. It was starting to feel like this could finally happen for us. After the excruciating two week wait, we found out we were pregnant. It was going to be a long 9 months ahead (with hearts full of cautious optimism) and I felt very vulnerable. The only thing I could cling onto was hope.

I don't want to skip over the fact that mentally and emotionally, I had come a long way up to this point. Right after losing Leo, I could not leave my house for a while. The sight of strollers, babies, children, and pregnant women – it was all so triggering. It was even difficult to watch movies or shows. You realize that everything in the world seemed to revolve around parenthood. I was also afraid to attend social events (and completely forget about any baby showers) even months after the loss, when I was attempting to be "normal" again. I feared the question that always gets asked when you're getting to know someone: "do you have kids?" I struggled with that question. I wanted to acknowledge Leo because he is my child (just not with me here on earth), yet I knew that talking about death would immediately make the other person feel regret for asking an "innocent" question. If I said, "not at the moment," the person would ask if we wanted children (yes, very much so, but obviously the world hates me) or they would launch into a monologue about how I should enjoy my time without kids and travel because their lives are too hectic with 3 rambunctious (healthy) children. So, going out into social situations outside of my close-knit circle, always seemed like a bad idea. Yet, I couldn't avoid it. I was forced to adjust and just let go of trying to make others comfortable with MY LOSS. It was kind of freeing. I was extremely over other people's comfort levels, their opinions, their questions, their theories on why my son passed away (mind you, these people did not hold a medical degree). I talked about Leo, and I did not shy away from the tough "innocent" questions. I wanted to normalize talking about motherhood and loss because it's a very lonely place for us mothers of angel babies. Yes, we are mothers too.

I am the mother of an angel baby boy and a sweet rainbow

baby who hopefully will one day understand just how much we wanted her in our lives. Motherhood is grief. Motherhood is joy. Above all, motherhood is love in various forms.

Ocean Vuong, a Vietnamese American poet and writer, once said in an interview (regarding the loss of his mother) that "Grief is perhaps the last and final translation of love . . . this is the last act of loving someone. And you realize that it will never end. You get to do this to translate this last act of love for the rest of your life."

These words really struck a chord with me. To me, looking back, motherhood felt like it began with deep sadness and grief. If grief is indeed an expression of love, then it's appropriate to say that my motherhood journey started with love and will end with love. The love for my children knows no bounds. My mother showed me that. Though my journey was not a smooth one, it is mine. It makes up the blueprint of my love for my children and any future child we may have. All the heartache has been worth the immense joy that I feel being a mother today. And to me, there is no greater gift.

If you've read my story thus far, thank you. I hope that my story will be able to reach and comfort those feeling isolated by grief and loss. You are not alone. Let me hold onto hope for you during a time where it is hard to find it for yourself.

CHAPTER 9

Angela

Growing up in a big Italian family I always dreamed of having a large family myself one day. You know just like the movies, where everyone would be super close, and we would have a Sunday Feast each week filled with laughter, love, and of course pasta. As the oldest of 4 children, most of my childhood was spent taking care of my sister and brothers. I cherished every moment and learned so much. I also never needed to ask for a "Betsy Wetsy" doll since I was always helping my mom change actual diapers.

I didn't meet my husband Michael until I was in my late 20s so when we finally said "I do" we started trying to expand our family even before our honeymoon ended. We were surprised how quickly we saw those two pink lines confirmed we were pregnant. Our pregnancy seemed like a breeze, and we were over the moon when we welcomed Lorenzo into the world weighing over 8 pounds. Shortly after Lorenzo's arrival we noticed he was not developing at the same rate as others in his play groups, and that he would very easily become agitated. Initially we were told not to worry, that "he would catch up." However, when he was about two, we noticed a few more behavioral issues which we discussed with his doctor in hopes of finding answers. We did get our answer, just one that we were not prepared to receive. Lorenzo was diagnosed with Autism. Getting this diagnosis took a huge emotional toll on us. On one hand we were happy to have a definitive answer but that feeling was fleeting as one by one more questions arose. We were fortunate to have a wonderful medical team to provide answers to our ongoing questions and even more fortunate to be able to provide Lorenzo with all the services he needed and continues to need to this day.

Michael and I really wanted to expand our family but I was struggling with what would be the best way.I was growing increasingly concerned for my age and I wanted to make sure I could continue to provide the much-needed support and extra attention my 5-year-old son, the center of my world, needed. After many prayers and meeting with our fertility specialist we decided to seek the help of a gestational surrogate. We were so blessed that our fertility clinic helped us connect with several potential surrogates. I will be honest it felt strange to interview "strangers" who were going to become family by giving us the ultimate gift, another child we could call our own. . When we met Catherine, we knew she would be the perfect surrogate. At our first meeting she was just so warm and had such a kind disposition, we easily and intuitively knew she was the perfect choice.

After our embryo was implanted, we had so many feelings running through our mind: anxious, excited, and hopeful. We were so thrilled when we heard our son's heartbeat on one of Catherine's first appointments. I was worried I would feel differently about my future son since this time I was not carrying him, but I never did. It was still love at first sight, well in this case love at first sound.

Throughout the entire pregnancy I would join Catherine for each doctor's appointment and of course during labor.

After just 12 hours of labor, our family was complete when little Matteo came out screaming like an opera singer. He is still pretty loud to this day. It is common to stay in touch with your gestational surrogate. However, Catherine continued to go above and beyond just staying in touch. She pumped breast milk for an entire year for Matteo! We still stay in contact to this day and send her updates on how our family is doing. Although not a blood relation, she will forever be our "family" having generously given us the most precious gift of all.

I always dreamt of a big family and my dreams have come true, although a little differently than I once thought. As for Sunday Feasts-they are even better than I could have imagined.

CHAPTER 10

Maureen

F reezing my eggs at 37

Even if you have the smallest inkling of a feeling that you may want children at some point, I encourage you to freeze your eggs. My only advice is to do it when you are young! "Young" is a funny word when you are talking about fertility and pregnancy, 35 is considered "old." Insane right? 35 is young in my opinion, when many women are in the prime of their life, balancing their careers and future aspirations. Results for egg retrieval is much better before the age of 35, so the earlier the better!

I started my journey at the age of 37. After my preliminary tests were very positive, my fertility specialist was very hopeful and confident that we would be successful and believed it would be an easy process despite being a little older.

If you have not been through this process let me tell you a little bit of what you can expect. During some of the initial testing, the specialist will see how many follicles you have, this will determine how many can and will potentially produce an egg. I had approximately 17, which was GREAT for someone my age as an over achiever I was excited.

Unfortunately, when we started the process my body wasn't responding to the fertility drugs like it was supposed to. After a few months of daily probing, prodding and of course monitoring the growth of my follicles, my big day was ALMOST here, retrieval day! I couldn't believe I was just a few days away. The anticipation was killing me, the best way I could describe it was when you are waiting for Christmas morning as a child. When I went for my final appointment before retrieval day we discovered that my follicles STILL were not responding like we hoped, and I only had 2 follicles.

Angry, paranoid and depressed that I was spending a lot of money and I MAY not get enough eggs for my theoretical one-day baby, I decided to see my acupuncturist for an extra visit. Throughout this entire process for me acupuncture was a great way to feel centered. As usual, when she listened to me it was so cathartic and just what I needed. I was raw and honest as I cried telling her how frustrated I was that my body was not reacting like my doctor, and I had hoped. Well, I am not quite sure what happened that day after my treatment but when I went to the doctor the next morning my follicles had grown larger overnight and there were even more popping up! It felt like literal MAGIC.

Retrieval day was finally here! When I came out of the surgery, the doctor told me they retrieved a WHOPPING 11 eggs, 8 of which were viable! Now although ideally, they would like 20 eggs this was great news for me because a few days earlier it was looking very grim. This process was a bit more stressful than I originally thought it would be, but it taught me a great deal on how resilient I truly am.

My Fertility specialist was not 100% confident 8 eggs would be enough to have a successful pregnancy, so he urged me to do another round sooner rather than later. He said he wanted 20 eggs total to feel "confident". I was just not emotionally ready for another round, yet.

Well, sooner ended up turning into later (about a year and half later) when I was 39.

Sadly, I was told that I was too late and I would likely not get enough eggs to freeze but that I would have more success if we went into a slightly different direction and freeze embryos. Now I felt defeated, I didn't have a partner that I wanted to make an embryo with, and I didn't want to use sperm from a sperm bank. I went into this process hoping that after I meet "the one" we could use my frozen eggs. I struggled making a decision, but with time and A LOT of thinking I decided not to complete a second round.

I wanted to share my story because I know there are women around the world just like me. If you are interested in preserving your fertility while you wait to meet the one or reach whatever personal and professional goals, you may have I urge you have open communication with your doctors. It doesn't have to be a taboo topic. Explore your options when you are in your late 20s or early 30s. Many young women can retrieve upwards of 20 or 30 eggs in one round! As you age the potential for having to complete more rounds is higher. With each round you have not only an increase in the financial costs but the emotional toll as well.

Afterword

JAMES CANGIALOSI

When I look for sources of strength, perseverance, humility, and spiritual connection, I am blessed not to look any farther than my wife, Julie.

Not long after we met in June 2009, I knew this woman with fire, passion, and determination to make the world a better place was my "one". Discussions of adventurous foreign travel, city living, marriage, and most importantly starting a family quickly followed. Our most exciting conversations focused on children, and our desire to become parents and share our love.

The realization of our dream of parenthood was not easy. Fortunately, our long and arduous journey towards becoming parents was ultimately successful.

Even as I count my current blessings, memories of sadness and helplessness seeing the love of my life suffer both physically and emotionally remain. During those dark and challenging times, we felt alone in our struggles. MOM, the personal accounts of others on the road to parenthood, was inspired by the need to address the isolation we experienced and give Hope to other couples currently facing fertility challenges.

We were able to meet exceptional people along this journey, including Nikki. Her contribution to this project as well as her friendship are a source of continued gratitude.

Acknowledgments

We would like to thank all the women who have so generously shared their experiences with us. Your strength in sharing your personal journey to motherhood is an inspiration to us all.

To the women and couples who will read this book, our hope is that these testimonials will remind you that you are not alone in your journey. WE see you; WE hear you, and WE are with you.

xo
Julie and Nikki

About the Contributing Author and Concept Creator Julie Cangialosi

Julie Cangialosi is a businesswoman, author, non-profit founder, and pageant queen.

Born in San Diego, California, she spent her formative years in Rhode Island, surrounded by her extended family. She grew up with a love for the arts which she expressed by singing and dancing with a local theatre company.

Julie is a Registered Dietitian, a graduate of Russell Sage College in Troy, NY, and has completed a Dietetic Internship at the University of Connecticut. She has been published in the Journal of the American Dietetic Association and is a member of The American Dietetic Association. Her science education led to a career as an Associate Director for a Pharmaceutical company.

In 2011 Julie married her husband James. They are the proud parents of Landon, Elle and 2 guardian angels. Their two pregnancy losses inspired their nonprofit Operation Little Angel 101: Hope After Loss. Julie has appeared on nationally syndicated talk shows and is a regular Today Show Parenting Teams contributor. When not championing her favorite causes, Julie and her family can be found traveling the world, visiting local museums, and cheering on the Washington Capitals!

About the Contributing Author and Concept Creator Nikki Noya

Nikki Noya is a Lifestyle Expert, Co-Host, and Executive Producer, On It Media

Nikki Noya was born in Newport Beach, California. She grew up playing volleyball, surfing, and swimming, activities that helped shape her career.

The former professional volleyball player is currently the Co-Host and Executive Producer at On It Media. She hosts the weekly nationally syndicated lifestyle and travel show, The Jet Set, alongside travel expert Booby Laurie.

Nikki obtained her BA in Communication degree from the University of Rhode Island, where she studied on a full volleyball scholarship. After graduation, she joined the AVP Next Pro Beach Beach Volleyball as a professional player.

Born of adventurous parents, Nikki also loved traveling since childhood. Her passion for sports, health, and adventure gradually morphed into media appearances. She started doing health and fitness segments on various news outlets, notably CNN.

She also shared her knowledge for healthy living and travel through her Fit to Fly segments on The Jet Set. These segments integrated travel and fitness, showcasing workouts, fitness-oriented vacations, and spa retreats.

Nikki joined the Jet Set TV team in 2016 as the lifestyle

expert, and thanks to her diligence and hard work, she became a co-host in 2018. Besides being a media personality and tv producer, she is a busy mom, beauty queen, author and philanthropist.

She is Vice president of Dress For Success Miami and Mrs. DC America 2019. She engages in a wide range of charitable causes through her family foundations. She would like to thank her husband for being at every single doctors appointment and her biggest supporter.